My
Ten Secrets
of Skiing

My Ten

Secrets of Skiing

By Bob Beattie

NEW YORK: THE VIKING PRESS

First published in 1968 by The Viking Press, Inc.
625 Madison Avenue, New York, N.Y. 10022

Published in conjunction with Eddie Elias Enterprises, Inc.

Published simultaneously in Canada by
The Macmillan Company of Canada Limited

Library of Congress catalog card number: 65-12026
Printed in U.S.A.

Acknowledgments

Many people have been of help to me in the preparation of this book, but without the help of two in particular the work would not have been possible—Dick Ericson and Doug Pfeiffer. Dick for his superb scratchboard renderings of the many skiing positions of the human body. Doug for his invaluable help in coordinating my convictions, developed while training and coaching America's greatest Alpine competitors, with the tenets of the Professional Ski Instructors of America.

I would also like to express thanks to the many individuals who compose the United States Ski Association, the National Ski Patrol System, Ski Industries of America, the Skiers' Training Trust, and the National Ski Areas Associations. Without the help of these agencies, I would not be able to achieve the goal of establishing America as one of the three leading competitive Alpine ski countries of the world.

BOB BEATTIE

v

Contents

Introduction

Bob Beattie, broad-shouldered, energetic, hard-driving, is the first man to come along with a complete program to put America on top of the competitive ladder in world Alpine ski competition. International race records show he is being successful.

During the 1964 Olympic Winter Games, three members of the Alpine squad which he coached brought home four Olympic medals. Two of these were men, and this was the first time that any male member of the U.S.A. squad had ever cracked the win-place-or-show barrier.

After five years of effort, Beattie succeeded in convincing the organizers of American ski racing that a positive program with continuity year after year, well-organized training camps, and high-caliber coaches—and a staggering budget of at least $177,000 annually—would be needed to achieve and maintain this goal.

He piled organizing success on top of organizing success, in spite of what his detractors originally called Beattie's "serious limitations." When he was appointed coach of the Alpine team for the 1962 World Championships in Chamonix, France, he was deemed incapable of dealing with the racing organizers because he was not from western Europe. He was called brash, bullying, the Ugly American. Yet, his tactics forced the Europeans, for the first time, to take the Americans seriously as a powerful Alpine skiing squad. His trainees skied victoriously for him, as he knew they would, and he won for America the respect from Europe which he was seeking.

Despite his team's 1962 successes, Beattie was held under fire back home. Many ski instructors ridiculed his invented terminology of ski technique. Such phrases as "go to the outside," "don't collapse the hips," "dynaturn" rankled many of them, especially the foreign-trained, who could not accept anything about skiing unless

Austria, Germany, or Switzerland had first espoused the idea. Beattie defended himself vigorously and convincingly. "Look," he said, "I'm a coach—my job is athletics, not physical-education instruction. I have to produce winning results. I work with great athletes from the start. I can take short cuts in producing results. In fact I *must* keep things simple, to the point, direct. An instructor's job is that of a teacher who has to explain the whys and wherefores of ski technique, and often to nonathletic types. In many respects, he has a tougher job than I have."

With proper usage, fire tempers iron to a steel-like hardness. When a man like Beattie has enough iron in him, pressure under fire only makes him stronger. Beattie has grown stronger during his relatively few years as the nation's top ski coach. He is now more penetrating, even more direct, in his approach to training racers. His directness is everywhere in this book. You will find it as helpful and rewarding to your skiing as I did while I helped Beattie to resolve any seeming contradictions between the problems of coaching athletes (top racers) and teaching P.E.—that is, instructing the recreational skier.

Savor Beattie's words carefully, study Dick Ericson's drawings closely, take lessons from a competent certified instructor, and surely you'll come out of the ranks of the average skier and end up with the experts.

Good luck!

> Doug Pfeiffer
> Editor in Chief of *Skiing* magazine
> Incorporating Director of the
> Professional Ski Instructors of America

My
Ten Secrets
of Skiing

The Story of Skiing

FOR ALL sports, competition—especially Olympic competition—is the research laboratory where the quest for greater speeds, greater safety, and better control over speed forge new designs in equipment and new methods in technique.

Skiing is no exception. In a very real sense, competitors themselves are the test pilots of the recreational sports world. I, as a coach, and they, as Olympic Alpine ski racers, are forever searching for every possible way to carve every one-hundredth of a second off the total time. On many occasions, the ski world's major downhill, slalom, and giant slalom races are won by just a few trifling split seconds. In an endless search for perfection, we inevitably discover simpler, faster, safer ways of carving a turn on skis.

The recreational skier gains from our search, of course. Through cooperation with the ski instructors, notably the Professional Ski Instructors of America, discoveries which are tried and proved in Olympic competition are distilled and codified into ways to teach the average recreational skier to ski more easily and more safely.

A look back at the development of Alpine ski racing and recreational Alpine skiing will show that this has always been true.

People have skied for thousands of years. Ancient skis found preserved in peat bogs of Scandinavia have been dated by modern

3

scientific processes at over four thousand years old. In several old books printed between 1550 and 1750, occasional references are made to people who glided over the snow while hunting wild game. A few ancient drawings depict Laplanders on long curved-up boards, with bows and arrows, showing that skis were used for hunting and probably for transportation over the frozen wastes of northern Europe and Asia.

As far as we know today, competition did not come to skiing until about the mid-1800s. In other words, for only a little over a hundred years has skiing been considered a sport, something with no direct relation to earning a living or keeping alive.

The first competitions that we know of were speed races held by Scandinavian forty-niners in the high mountain snow and gold fields of California and jumping events in Norway, amusing accounts of which appear in a few old ski books.

Apparently in the late 1800s a spirit of competition arose between the husky young men of two Norwegian towns, Christiania (now Oslo) and Telemark. Incidentally, these names still serve in the vocabulary of today's skiers; both refer to the turns which skiers make. Though a Telemark is now considered to be an obsolete way of turning, all skiers are familiar with the word "christie," which is short for Christiania. The spirit of competition between the two towns spurred local craftsmen to make better equipment, and the better the equipment became the more daring were the Norwegian jumpers. Even today, Norway prides itself in being the world's leader in developing Olympic jumping champions. And when the world famous Holmenkollen event is held annually, well over a hundred thousand spectators attend, including the King of Norway.

Today, there are two basic types of skiing competition: Alpine and Nordic. Alpine events are essentially down-mountain races, the familiar slalom, giant-slalom, and downhill races. Nordic events are cross-country races of varying distances (up to fifty kilometers, or just over thirty-one miles) and jumping events. In this book, we are concerned with Alpine skiing, the kind of skiing which has captured the imagination and love of millions of people all over the world wherever snow and hills make the sport a possibility.

Alpine skiing takes its name from the mountains where this sport developed—the Alps of Europe, notably in Austria, Switzerland, and France. Even in these countries, the original interest in and growth of the sport have resulted from competition. After experimenting for some years in his native Austria, Matthias Zdarsky issued a defiant challenge to anyone from Norway to try to outski him on the steep, heavily snow-covered slopes of the Alps. Zdarsky used only one long stick for a ski pole. With it, he was able to make a sort of pole-vaulted turn on hard snow and, by leaning heavily upon it to one side or the other, to make an awkward turn with his skis in a snowplow position. Zdarsky focused attention upon skiing as a feasible winter recreation in the European Alps. His keen competitive spirit spurred him to invent several ski bindings and skis which were more suited for Alpine skiing than were the cross-country and jumping equipment of the Norwegians.

Sir Arnold Lunn, the renowned British chronicler of skiing history and inventor of the slalom race, says that in 1892, when the first of the now famous Holmenkollen events were held near Christiania, the races were quite different from those of today. The races were downhill in nature, since none of the racers could turn, and there were many obstacles throughout the course, such as jumps over sheds or over the small dams of water ponds. Each racer used one long stick, instead of ski poles, which was used to make a sort of pole-vaulted turn or put between the legs and sat upon when a stop was necessary. The other favorite method of stopping was to fall.

For a period roughly between 1900 and 1920, the methods of Zdarsky and the Telemark turn and the Christiania turn of the Norwegians dominated Alpine skiing. These were gradually replaced, however, by methods developed by several Austrians, most notable of whom was Hannes Schneider.

Hannes Schneider was born and raised in a humble Austrian

village called Saint Anton am Arlberg. He devised certain improvements in skiing techniques, especially the stem turn and stem Christiania, and is credited with being the first man to evolve a commercially acceptable ski-school system. Not only that, he was a great competitor and usually won his victories by considerable margins. His fame attracted to Saint Anton British vacationers, who came to learn how to ski in his schools. Schneider's ability to ski, to organize, and to teach led him to become known as the founder of the Arlberg system of skiing.

The Arlberg system dominated the skiing world for forty years and is largely responsible for the early growth and popularity of the sport. With various modifications, this system held sway until as late as 1955. Many factors influenced the Arlberg system, however, and some of the modifications to Schneider's original concept were considerable. The most notable changes were the direct products of two great skiers—the first, Anton Seelos; the second, Emile Allais.

Toni Seelos was an Austrian skier who, around 1930, began to win virtually every race he entered. Seelos skied without using a stemming movement. He had mastered the technique of making parallel christies, something which skiers had talked of for years as being the ultimate in skiing efficiency, but something which somehow had previously defied execution.

A keen-minded Frenchman, Emile Allais, who was later to become several times the World Champion skier, was quick to realize the efficiency of Seelos's racing technique. Under Seelos's tutelage, Allais mastered this revolutionary style and began to win most of Europe's major races. Thrilled with his successes, Allais set himself the task of distilling this new racing technique into a method of instruction suitable for teaching anyone who wanted to learn the sport.

Allais's theories stimulated racers, week-end skiers, and the ski industry alike. Manufacturers of ski equipment, now understanding better the technical needs of ski racing, produced a remarkable amount of more efficient equipment: faster skis, harder and

6

sharper steel edges, safer and stronger ski bindings, and ski boots so well made that they transmitted exactly to the ski the slightest movement of the skier's foot and ankle.

Allais's revolutionary approach to ski teaching favorably influenced the world's ski instructors as well. His exposé of the basic skills needed for skiing well, for skiing fast and safely—namely, sideslipping, unweighting, and a rotational force—enabled other countries of the world to develop great competitors. Some of these, who in turn influenced the week-end skiers' pleasure, were Switzerland's Rudi Rominger, Norway's Stein Eriksen, and Italy's Zeno Colo.

France took the lion's share of wins in the big international competitions of Europe between 1936, when Emile Allais won his first World Champion title, and 1950. In the Olympics of 1952, Stein Eriksen was crowned World Champion skier. He has since retired from competition. An active member of the Professional Ski Instructors of America, he keeps busy passing on to pleasure skiers many of the secrets which made him so great.

To the discerning observer at the 1952 Olympics, the new crop of postwar racers skied with a new zest, with greater skill, with a greater ability to turn quickly and almost instantly. Known as a superb all-round athlete, Eriksen exemplified this new technique. But so did many of the world's great Alpine racers, especially a group of speedy Austrians.

By the time of the 1956 Olympics, a clear-cut revolution in ski techniques had taken place. An almost unbelievably good Austrian racer, Toni Sailer, won all three Alpine events, a feat never before, and never since, duplicated. Furthermore, the Austrians, under the leadership of Professor Stefan Kruckenhauser, were the first to analyze and systematize the new techniques of the elite racers into a way of teaching them to the recreational skier. The technique, popularly known as wedeln, has now captured the fancy of the skiing world.

Once again the fruits of competition were made available for the enjoyment of the nonracer.

Refinements in the design and manufacture of ski equipment, especially American-made equipment, have continued since that time. So too have refinements and changes in ski techniques and ski instruction. For example, in January 1965, the Professional Ski Instructors of America presented a demonstration to the Seventh Annual World Ski School Congress which brought recognition of United States instructors as among the world's leaders in ski teaching.

American Alpine ski racers, such as Bud Werner, Jim Heuga, Bill Kidd, Bill Marolt, and Jean Saubert, have proved that we can produce ski racers who must be rated with the world's best.

My experiences in coaching the cream of American competitive skiers and observing at close quarters all of the world's elite during their training and actual racing have made me very much aware of these improvements. It is my hope, in this book, to pass on some of them for the benefit and enjoyment of America's growing number of pleasure-seeking skiers.

The Ten Secrets of Skiing

I DECIDED to become a full-time ski coach after the disappointing showing made by our Olympic Alpine skiers at the 1960 Winter Games held in Squaw Valley, California. I pondered the reasons for our continued lack of success, and they gradually became obvious to me.

We had no national team, no national coach, no regular training —in fact, we had no system of organization whatsoever. Sure, the National Ski Association (now called the United States Ski Association) organized the races, but nobody really organized the racers nor trained them, to make victory on the international circuit a possibility.

I set for myself the task of doing just that—setting up, carrying out, and maintaining a program for our ski racers which would at long last put the United States among the world's best. The record book shows that we are making good progress.

I don't intend to go into the organizational details of this plan. My purpose in this book is to bring to you those things, those maneuvers—the secrets, as it were—which I recognized as being basic to developing skiers capable of winning Olympic medals.

It has been my fortunate pleasure, as coach of the United States FIS (Fédération Internationale du Ski) Alpine Team, and the Olympic team, to have been able to work with our country's best skiers.

9

But even they are sometimes handicapped by improper techniques they may have learned in their early days. Because I am no expert in the art of teaching beginners, nor even intermediates, I have relied heavily upon the experience of Doug Pfeiffer to make my approach practical for newcomers to the sport. Doug is one of the founders of the American Technique and the Professional Ski Instructors of America and has been responsible for the teaching of thousands of skiers, not to mention the early training of some of our National Ski Team members.

Through the years, I have studied miles and miles of slow-motion movies of the best slalomers and downhillers to be found anywhere. I soon realized that they all skied with very definite and very similar movements. The consistent winners, more especially, skied with a great economy of motion and a tremendous sense of balance. Undoubtedly, these racers were born with a good balance, and years of practice improved and developed it. But I believe firmly that they ski with such good balance because of their ability to ski accurately. That is to make no movement which would throw them off balance—because they make only the necessary, correct movements to begin with.

There is really nothing too revolutionary in my approach to developing great skiers. But I do stress systematic development. And I do like to keep things simple. I believe there is a definite basic way to ski, especially to ski for racing, and that basic way is what this book is about. Throughout, you'll notice I lay great stress on keeping forward and on keeping your weight toward the outside of a turn. If there is any one thing, any one overriding secret of skiing, it's this business of keeping forward. But more on that topic in later pages.

THE FIRST SECRET:

Getting in Shape

You cannot ski if your body is not ready for the task. To ski, especially to ski well and with maximum safety, you must get in shape and keep in shape. Ski instructors the world over have told me that one of the big problems in trying to teach people is that many of them do not have the strength even to lift themselves off the snow. Nor do they have the endurance to ski for more than an hour or so without becoming too fatigued to progress properly. This is especially true in the West, where the beginner must often learn at elevations above eight thousand feet. Realize, too, that skiing takes place out of doors, sometimes in very cold weather, and that you are encumbered with an extra twenty to thirty pounds of equipment. You bet skiing can be strenuous—but not impossibly so, for people from three to eighty-three, even ninety-three, ski.

Once your body is in shape, skiing helps to maintain your condition, provided you ski often enough—say each week end during the winter. But what about the other six to nine months? You must do something to prevent muscles from turning to flab—or to build up muscles which you never had.

When training Olympic skiers, I use what is often referred to as "the exhaustion method." This consists of working the trainees, who are in their late teens and early twenties, until they think they are exhausted. But we keep the pressure on them even then, almost forcing them to the very limits of their endurance. The idea here is to make them realize that the human body can endure much more punishment than anyone usually believes possible. This breeds in our racers a sense of confidence, a knowledge that during a race they can overcome any obstacle of physical endurance in order to win. Our racers are tough. They must keep tough and get tougher.

But as for you, a recreational skier, what can you use as a yardstick for physical fitness?

If you follow, for example, the Royal Canadian Air Force program for your age bracket, you will be extremely fit for skiing, as well as for all other sports.

One of the best exercises I know of for all-around conditioning is running. Start off on short jaunts to begin with, and gradually increase the distance to two or three miles. Do this three times a week, starting about the middle of September, and you'll be able to cope with almost any situation on the slope.

The sight of a man or woman running down the streets of Suburbia in the early morning or evening could provoke onlookers into calling the police to investigate this suspicious character. Running through the streets of Metropolia might also prove hazardous. If running is out of the question for you, I have an exercise—or really a series of exercises—which can be performed in most homes and which I use extensively in training champion-caliber skiers. These exercises are performed with equipment used also by championship-class boxers and children alike; a jump rope! Just a simple, inexpensive seven-foot length of carpenter's sash cord can provide the average person with just about all the equipment he needs to get in better-than-average shape.

Jumping rope has, for training skiers, the decided advantage of developing excellent hand-eye-feet coordination. This type of coordination is vital for skiers who must learn to look where they intend to be in a split second or so, while at the same time planting the ski pole and turning the skis. Also, rope jumping—skipping, if you prefer—develops the lungs and endurance, reduces weight, and builds smooth, fast-working muscles over much of the body.

Our Olympic trainees were quick to invent a variety of fancy footwork exercises while skipping rope, patterned after some of the modern rock-'n'-roll dances. An excellent little book has been written on the subject, with illustrations of many jump variations. You can get it by sending a dollar to Professor F. B. Prentup, Colorado University, Boulder, Colorado.

But jumping rope might knock loose the plaster on the ceiling of the apartment below you, or break chandeliers and furniture; perhaps a wife or husband may stand in your way. Then your only alternative, if you don't play some other strenuous sport, such as tennis, is to resort to calisthenics. Your best bet, of course, is to join a physical-fitness program with an athletic club or commercial gym or a Y. Working out with others makes the effort more sociable and provides incentive to keep up your fitness program.

Here is a brief list of the parts of the body which must be exercised and strengthened for skiing, and some exercises to do the job:

The Calves. Toe-risers: Place a thick phone book under the toes, reaching to the ball of the foot, then repeatedly rise up to stand on your toes. This exercise is especially important for girls who have worn high heels for years. Ultimately, repeat at least twenty-five times.

The Thighs. Keeping the knees and feet together, with feet flat on the floor, do knee-bends as you can. Ultimately, at least twenty-five. Also practice the "Phantom Chair" until you can hold the position for at least one or two minutes: Planting your feet firmly on the floor, lean your back against a wall and lower yourself into the position you would take if you were sitting in a straight-backed chair.

The Back, Hips, Waist, and Torso. Any variety of trunk-bending exercises (forward-backward; side-to-side; in circles) will help to roll off your spare tire, stretch seldom-used muscles, and generally loosen up the torso so as to greatly reduce the possibility of pulled muscles while skiing. Everyone should be able to perform at least fifty leg-lifts and fifteen to twenty-five sit-ups. For sit-ups, keep the knees bent and either hook your feet under a heavy piece of furniture, such as a bed, or have someone hold your feet down.

The Arms and Shoulders. For beginners, the arms and shoulders play a frequent role in helping to return to an upright standing position. For expert skiers, the arms must be strong to use the ski poles effectively while making christies. One of the best ex-

13

ercises for developing arms and shoulders is the familiar push-up. Ladies should do these with their knees on the floor but their backs kept straight. Men whose arms can no longer lift their bodies, should also use the ladies' method until they can keep the knees off the floor. To be in shape for skiing, you should be able to do at least twenty of the ladies' push-ups, ten of the men's.

When you keep your body in good physical condition, aside from the all-round benefits of healthful living, you enjoy a three-way skiing benefit: first, your increased endurance permits you to ski more hours of the day and to do more maneuvers; second, rough falls do no more than shake you up for a few moments—your chances of sustaining serious or painful injury when in good shape are very much reduced; third, because of your awareness of the slim chance of injury, you gain great confidence and lose a great deal of fear, so that you soon ski with a new-found sense of freedom.

Is it any wonder, then, that I consider being in shape the first secret of enjoyable skiing?

THE SECOND SECRET:

Proper Equipment

If the first secret of skiing is being in shape then the second is having the proper tools with which to work. The tools in this case are not only skis, boots, poles, and bindings, but clothing as well. Keep in mind that when you are exercising, you generate up to sixteen times as much heat as when you are passive. That's a tough challenge for clothing to meet, since you may have to work hard climbing the ski-lift ramp only to sit passively in the cold for ten to fifteen minutes on the lift.

But high-quality ski clothing can meet the challenge easily. Let's start from the skin out, remembering that several layers of lightweight items are warmer than one bulky item. Start with long underwear, preferably the thermal variety; a pair of light wool or silk socks with a pair of heavy rag-wool "Norwegian" socks; and a T shirt with a turtle neck that can be rolled up when the weather is really nippy.

Stretch ski pants are next. The warmest have a high wool count. The best stretch fabrics are heavier, warmer, shed water better, hold their shape better, and protect legs from bruises better than the less expensive, high-count rayon pants.

Choose a sweater to suit your tastes. If the weather is below ten degrees, you might want to wear a warm shirt over the T shirt. I find that the lightweight shirts of nylon (skiers call them nylon shells) keep in a great deal of warmth. Cardigans are more versatile, since they can be unbuttoned when you get too warm.

Ski parkas are warmest when they extend at least to the wrist. Many of the synthetic-fiber fills which have been invented recently are excellent in providing warmth without weight. Ounce for ounce, however, nothing beats good-quality down feathers as filler. Parkas with hoods, either concealed or not, add versatility to your clothing. Wristlets—preferably not of wool, which only

15

causes snow to cling to them—help keep the hands warm. Your parka will be even more adaptable to your changes in heat output if it contains a two-way zipper. On snowy days, working out on the slopes with the team, I often work up quite a heat. By undoing the zipper from the bottom up, I am able to keep cool air circulating around my torso, while keeping the snow from getting in at my chest.

All types and styles of gloves are now available for the skier. Fingered gloves give a better grip on the ski pole but are not as warm as the old-fashioned mitts. Some skiers find that gloves lined with two layers of Curon, a foam insulator, are warm enough for all but sub-zero skiing. On those days, even wearers of mitts add an extra layer of silk or wool liners.

Oddly enough, if you suffer from cold feet and fingers, you may solve your problem by wearing a warm hat. That's because the heart always makes sure the brain gets the warmest supply of blood. If you are not wearing a hat, a great deal of your precious body heat will escape out the top, so to speak.

Certain accessories are indispensable, such as sunglasses and foul-weather goggles. At high altitudes, say over a mile, more than twenty-five per cent of the sun's ultraviolet rays can cause temporary injury to the retina of your eye. Goggles are needed, of course to see when the skiing's often the best—namely, when it's blizzardy. An experienced skier or a specialty ski-shop operator can advise you about which type is least likely to fog.

Clothing, the right clothing, insures your comfort and makes skiing more pleasurable as a consequence. But no matter how comfortable you are, you will not be able to ski well unless you have suitable boots. Of all the paraphernalia needed for skiing, nothing is more important than boots designed and built for the job. Then you need the best of release bindings, then good skis and poles.

But how to know what's good or what's bad? Over a hundred different models of ski boots are available on the market and almost as many different models of skis. I cannot answer this question to your complete satisfaction here, but I can give you some positive suggestions. First, deal with reputable shops which specialize in ski equipment and which are known for their integrity. Certainly, you may find bargains at discount houses or department stores, but you should very definitely know your merchandise, especially when bargain shopping.

Almost all ski instructors recommend that you rent your equipment for your first two or three forays to the ski area. Without question, you will learn much about equipment, where to shop, etc. You will become more aware of your individual needs and become especially aware of what to look for, in terms of fit and value, when it comes to buying your ski boots. This item should be your first big purchase for the sport and should account for a good portion of your budget, unless you are lucky enough to find someone with good used boots in your exact size for a reasonable price.

Quality ski boots do not come cheap. The very best, which are not recommended for beginners' use, cost over a hundred twenty-five dollars. Anything much less than thirty dollars new is getting on the cheap side of things; forty-five to sixty is a safe range. Always walk around the shop for several moments with both boots on. Always try them on with the same type of thick socks that you would ski with. Make sure that your toes can wiggle slightly. This is important to keep your feet warm. Be sure that your heel does not slip up more than the merest fraction of an inch when someone holds the heel of the boot to the floor and you lean forward, hard. Shop for your boots. Try on several brands in your size and several of the same size in the brand you finally choose. A specialty ski shop should have a device for making minor stretching adjustments in the boot of your choice to insure a comfortable fit.

Good boots are extremely important, because they are a major part of the link between you and your skis. Your boots should give an almost plaster-cast-like support to the side of your ankles, providing safety and superior control over the edges of your skis, while in no way interfering with the normal forward-bending ability of your ankle.

Another major link between you and your skis is the binding. Here too, the issue is confusing because so many bindings are now available. You should rely on the experience of good skiing friends or the advice of a good ski shop. In any event, unless you are an expert, stay away from the so-called long-thong type of binding. Be sure that you get a binding which allows for a direct, forward- or backward-fall release—in addition to a twist release—since most falls occur with a combination of these two movements. Expect to pay at least fifteen dollars for your bindings, and learn thoroughly how to adjust them yourself. Bindings do come out of adjustment, so you should test them first thing every day you ski and reset them if necessary to insure your own safety. The best binding is only as good as its adjuster, so take time to know what you are doing.

Advising a nonskier on what boot to buy is difficult, because only he can tell if the fit is exact, or if the discomfort is major or minor.

While the selection of skis is every bit as involved as the selection of boots, at least there are several rules to go by which makes the task easier. For instance, what length of ski? For the first two or three times you rent them, preferably not much longer than your height. Thereafter, for girls, not much more than three inches longer than their height; for men, not much more than six inches longer. Racers select the length in accordance with the needs of the event, but in no event are skis more than one foot longer than the skier's height.

If you are heavy for your height, you should have a stiff model. If average in weight, then choose a standard flex ski. If you are a lightweight, then seek a soft, very flexible model. All skis should have about one and a half to two inches of camber—that is, when they are laid bottom-to-bottom, the arch between them at the middle should not exceed two inches.

What model of skis should you get? Unless you are a racer—or an expert, in which event you'll know what you need—don't buy racing skis. They will be too difficult for you to enjoy, since they are designed for high speed and very strong legs.

What material? Epoxy plastic? Metal? Wood? That's a tough question. Metal skis are excellent and last for years. On the other hand, the epoxy skis, the so-called plastic or fiber-glass skis, tend to be easier for the learning skier and the intermediate to handle. Many experts use them too, though up to now they have not been nearly as durable as the metal skis. Virtually none but the cheapest of skis are made entirely of wood today. While these skis do ski well, they are subject to warpage, breakage, and rapid wear. Skis priced between twenty-five and forty dollars seldom last for more than two seasons of week-end use, and that's with good care. Skis in the fifty-to-eighty-dollar bracket are generally much superior and should provide at least three or four good seasons of recreational use. Above the eighty-dollar price, skis become superior in quality, though the best metal skis sell for a hundred and up. And epoxy skis range around two hundred.

Because of the complicated nature of the situation, you can see why it is advisable to rent equipment for your first few trips, and then to rely on help from ski instructors, knowledgeable friends, and reputable ski shops. Each purchase is such an individual matter that your personal needs and budget must be taken into serious consideration.

One item of ski equipment remains to be discussed. Ski poles. It's hard to go wrong here, provided you stay in the better quality price range—eight to fifteen dollars is a good guide. As for length, a long pole reaches your armpit when you are standing; a short one come to your waist. Choose a length halfway between.

A final word on equipment. When you are learning to ski, it is difficult to know whether your skiing problems may be a direct result of faulty equipment. A knowledgeable certified ski instructor is trained to spot such problems. The wrong equipment can make a misery of your ski time—one good argument for taking lessons.

Believe me, the better you ski, the better your equipment must be, and the worse your equipment, the longer it will take you to become a better skier.

THE THIRD SECRET:

The Basics

Basic to any sport is prior familiarization with that sport's implements. You must become accustomed to handling the tools of the sport. When you are first on skis, you find they make you very awkward. You feel strange when trying to coordinate the movement of your arms, which are holding onto fifty-inch poles, with the movements of your feet, which seem to be tethered to seventy-two-inch planks.

The task can be very trying and no fun at all unless you go about it in the right way. I wholeheartedly endorse the idea that you take lessons from a certified teacher who can teach you correctly. In fact, that idea itself is, without question, a very important secret of learning to ski quickly, easily, and safely.

I'll make that point even stronger: Don't try to learn to ski without the aid of a certified teacher. He or she can teach you in the first few hours what it would take a whole book to explain. For that reason, I am cutting to the barest essentials my descriptions of the early fundamentals of skiing. Do them right and you'll have little trouble learning. Do them wrong and you'll need much effort—plus the experienced eye of an instructor to set you right.

The basics that I'm talking about here are those involved in getting ready to ski downhill, the so-called static maneuvers of skiing. They are: walking, falling, getting up, climbing, step turns, and the kick turn.

Walking

Walking

One of the first rules in learning to ski is this: Spend at least one hour of your first attempt practicing on perfectly flat ground. You must learn to walk on skis, to be able to swing them straight ahead in line with the direction in which you want to go. And you must coordinate your arm movement with the leg motion.

The basic body movement is the same as that for walking without skis, except that you make adjustments for the long extensions on your arms and legs. As you study the illustrations, notice the following points:

1. I look straight ahead, in the direction I want to go.

2. My left foot is forward, and so is my left knee. I have taken a long step, having pushed off my right ski.

3. My right arm has been brought forward to balance the movement of my left leg. *Important:* Note that I do not plant my ski pole ahead of my leading foot. My ski poles always slant backward, even when I reach forward, so that I can get a strong push with each one. This push helps me to get a good glide of several feet.

4. My skis nearly always glide on the snow. I do not try to pick them up with each step, although it is not critical if their tails do lift off as the result of an especially long stride or strong push.

Falling

There is a right way to fall safely and there are many wrong ways. The problem of falling becomes more serious the faster you move. As good a time as any to learn to fall is when you are not even sliding. The idea is to fall backward by lowering your hips (your seat) but not to sit directly backward. That would only make you into an out-of-control toboggan, with you sitting on the tails of your skis, heading for the obstacle you wanted to avoid. After you've sat backward for some distance, twist your seat toward one side of the slope or the other, keeping your knees somewhat up in the air. You may use your hands to help soften your landing, as I am doing in Dick Ericson's illustration of falling.

Falling

Getting Up

I mentioned earlier that getting up takes strength in the upper body. The task is much easier once you've learned to follow these simple rules.

1. Make sure your skis are on the low side of the slope. In other words, they should be lower than your seat, if you are on a slight slope.

2. Get your skis parallel and bring them fairly close to your seat. Be sure that the skis are in such a position (across the hill), so that they will not slide either forward or backward once you try to stand up.

3. Place your ski poles as I have done in the first drawing. Note that I removed my hands from the straps, and, in the side view (drawing 2), see how my poles again slant backward so that I can pull myself up-and-forward.

4. I pull myself up with the upper hand, while pushing with the lower. I must keep my hips forward enough so that my center of gravity, which is somewhere low in the center of my waist, is kept ahead of my heels. Note in the second drawing how my lower hand has "walked" up the poles as I have raised myself.

Now that you are on your feet, fall down again, the safe way. Now get up. Practice this three or four times to help fix in your mind the proper procedure.

Getting up after fall—front view

Getting up after fall—side view

25

Climbing

To pull a switch on an old phrase, what comes down must first go up. Lifts and tows have made climbing almost a lost art, but no skier worthy of the name can get by without having to do some climbing each ski day. Besides, walking or climbing on skis helps you develop much of the coordination you'll need to keep your skis under control on the way down. There are three basic climbing steps:

Side-stepping. Side-stepping is the easiest way to climb short steep slopes. It's like climbing a stairway sideways. First you move one ski, the uphill ski (which is the higher of the two), about a foot sideways, keeping it parallel to the lower ski. Note how I have cocked my uphill knee and ankle to give me a somewhat bowlegged look. This action insures that the uphill edge of my uphill ski will firmly grip the snow. This "edging" of the ski gets increasingly important the harder and icier the snow becomes.

Next, simply bring the lower ski up to within a few inches of the upper ski, making sure you slam the uphill edge of the lower ski into the snow. Repeat till you get where you're going.

Diagonal Side Step. Imagine you are walking up a wide flight of museum steps at an angle to them. If you were on skis, you'd be using what is called the diagonal side step, except that as you move each foot sideways you also move it forward. This method of climbing is most suitable when you are making long climbs up almost any slope. First you would traverse up the slope in one direction, make a kick turn, then continue to use the diagonal side step to traverse upward in the other direction.

Side-stepping

27

Diagonal Side Step

The Herringbone. Look at the way I am climbing in this illustration. Can you visualize that the tracks I leave behind would look much like the backbone and ribs of a well-deboned fish? That's why the maneuver is called the herringbone. This way of climbing requires good coordination and is very useful for quick but short climbs. Here, once again, as in walking, my ski poles are never planted ahead of my leading foot. See how my skis are slammed to the snow on their inside edges.

The Herringbone

29

The Step Turns

An easy way to make a marked change of direction on the flat is with the step turns. There are two types, one in which the tips of the skis are left in place, and the other in which the heels of the skis remain more or less in place, as shown in the drawing. The movements are simple.

In the first kind of step turn, simply pick up the heel of one ski, leaving the tip on the snow, and move the ski sideways in a rotary fashion, as if you were trying to describe a pie-shaped wedge with your skis. Then bring the other ski alongside. Repeat the process until you have turned the desired amount.

The second kind of step turn is done the same way, the only difference being that the heels of the skis are kept on the snow to act as pivots for the action. *Caution:* Do not take steps that are too wide, or you might cross your skis.

The Step Turn

The Kick Turn

This turn, although a bit complicated, allows you to make a quick about-face. It comes in handy for traversing up a slope or for coming down a slope too steep for you to make fast turns.

Starting with both skis together, on a perfectly flat spot, kick up one ski as I have done. Note that I have already started to fold over my turning ski so that it will rest alongside the other ski, pointing in its new direction. Then I simply bring the other ski around. You can make many minor mistakes when learning this maneuver. So, again, you would do well to be supervised by a competent teacher when you try.

The Kick Turn

THE FOURTH SECRET:

Fall-Line Maneuvers

The fourth secret is really basic, really vital, to your skiing progress. If you don't successfully master these fall-line maneuvers (straight running and snowplowing), you will never be able to ski with the complete freedom and precise control of an expert. From now on, skiing becomes dynamic, active, and forever exciting.

The fall line is described in the official manual of the Professional Ski Instructors of America as "The line of the slope; the imaginary line down a slope which a rolling ball would trace. The most direct way straight down the immediate slope upon which you stand."

Straight Running

The head-on illustration shows the basic position used for skiing straight down the fall line. Chin up, eyes looking twenty to thirty feet ahead. Feet are a comfortable couple of inches apart, so that each ski is in direct line under its corresponding leg and hip. The arms are slightly bent at the elbows and held slightly away from the body, to give better sideways balance. In short, my body is directly centered over both skis.

Now take a close look at the side view. Notice the easy flex of the ankles, knees, and waist. This position is what Doug Pfeiffer calls balanced stance. It is the best stance I know of for all skiers. Notice how the body appears to lean forward slightly. It actually does, and my weight rests almost entirely on the ball of each foot, where it must if I am to prevent myself from falling over backward every time the snow gets a bit faster or the slope a bit steeper.

From this position of balanced stance, your legs, by flexing more or less at the knees and ankles, can immediately absorb most

34

variations in snow and slope. Also, by moving the hips and shoulders more forward, a great deal of pressure can be applied to the front of the skis, as in the second side view. This forward pressure, or forward lean, is indispensable, when used properly, for advanced skiing. But we'll get to that soon.

Straight Running Position—head on

35

Straight Running Position—side view

Pronounced Forward Lean

The Snowplow

Straight running is a means of going faster. The snowplow, which we'll talk about now, is a means of slowing down and, on gentler slopes, a way to come to a stop.

In the head-on drawing, note that once again the body remains centered over both skis. The skis have been pushed out into a V position, so that they rest lightly on their inside edges. In part, the degree to which the edges are angled to the snow controls my speed. By pulling my knees together slightly, causing my ankles to roll inward a bit, I cause the skis to edge more. This slows me down. I can slow down more effectively once I learn to widen the V by pushing my heels farther apart and then edging more. To go faster, simply reverse the process. That is, edge less and narrow the V.

The side view of the snowplow reveals how I maintain balanced stance even though my skis are V'd.

Caution: Too much unsupervised practice of the snowplow, or its practice to the exclusion of other maneuvers, can cause you to develop bad habits which will get in the way of your rapid learning progress for years to come.

Snowplow—head on

Snowplow—side view

THE FIFTH SECRET:

Traversing

Two body positions are basic to all good skiing. We've had one of them: straight running. The other is traversing.

Before going any further, I want to elaborate on the phrase "body positions." Do not get the notion that you are to assume these positions correctly and then hold them for all skiing. The American Technique points out two basic principles which apply here: total motion and natural positions.

Working hand and glove, these two concepts explain that skiing positions are not static, that "positions" are really simply a convenient way of showing the average position of the body at most times while skiing. The body must be constantly and totally in motion at all times, even though the movements are barely perceptible.

It is this subtle motion—call it rhythm, if you want, or elegant rhythm—which makes for good skiing. With practice, the rhythmic subtlety develops. What I'm trying to say here is this: "Don't freeze into rigid position while skiing. Stay loose."

Now, the traverse position. Traversing means skiing across a hill or across the fall line. Since every good turn must start from a traverse position, be assured that if that position, for no matter how short a moment it is assumed, is not correct, the turn will not develop properly.

Traversing on gentle slopes of soft-packed snow requires a position similar to straight running, especially when viewed head on. Note that because the upper ski is slightly higher than the lower, so too are the following uphill parts of the body: the knee, the hip, and the shoulder. Note how the skis rest on their uphill edges.

Traverse—head on

Traverse—side view

From the side, you can see at a glance that traversing requires the upper ski to be slightly advanced. Correspondingly, the uphill knee, hip, and shoulder are advanced by the same amount.

This body position should be natural and not forced. The position becomes more noticeable the steeper the slope becomes and the harder the snow gets. On a very steep slope, the shoulders should be turned so that they are actually parallel to the slope, with the upper body leaning away from the hill. This shoulder action counteracts the movement of the knees into the hill. Such a position of angulation allows you to get a firm grip on the snow, either to hold your direction of traverse or to carve a tight turn.

The proper amount of angulation (namely, no more than is needed for the purpose) also makes it easier for you to keep more weight on your lower ski, where it belongs. The proper weight distribution is about seventy per cent on the lower, thirty per cent on the upper.

Many instructors have told me that too many pupils practice too little traversing to ever become consistently good skiers. After spending years trying to develop racers out of some of our better teen-age skiers, I can believe it. Even an Olympic champion could not win ski races if he did not know the secret of angulation—the key to proper traversing.

THE SIXTH SECRET:
Sideslipping

The ability to let your skis move sideways, instead of just forward in the direction which they point, is indeed a major secret of modern skiing. A good skier knows how to sideslip—not only forward, but backward as well. However, the most important form of sideslipping is a curving sideslip. All of our modern racing turns—the christies—consist basically of two actions: first to start yourself skidding, then to control that skid so as to carve on the snow a curve of whatever degree you desire.

The importance of sideslipping was not really recognized until Emile Allais figured it out as a basic component of a parallel christie. He devised many exercises to help people learn this skill. He pointed out that it was most important for people to learn to handle the peculiar side-to-side balance (lateral balance) necessary to vary the sharpness of turns.

Controlling a skid, a sideslip, is a matter of delicate control with the ankles and the knees. The more lateral support your boots provide, the less work the ankles have to do and the more precisely you can control your edges, which in turn control the sideslip.

Here's the idea. Supposing you are standing across the hill in a normal traverse position, with a slight amount of angulation. Your skis, as a consequence, are edged. They cannot slip sideways. Now, if you stand up straighter so that you lose some of your angulation, your knees will move away from the hill and tend to release the grip of your edges on the snow. At this point, your skis will want to move sideways. If they don't, you may have to roll your ankles slightly away from the hill to further release your edges, as the drawing shows. Let your whole body slide sideways with the movement of your feet and you will sideslip in balance. This type of sideslipping is called lateral sideslip and is more of an exercise than a practical maneuver, although any good skier finds the exercise has its practical uses from time to time.

The handiest form of sideslipping, because it is closely related to a parallel christie, is a curving sideslip. To learn this, let's start with an exercise called diagonal sideslipping. Here's how.

On a smooth-packed slope, about twenty degrees in steepness, begin traversing in a good natural position of angulation. After a few feet, release the grip of your edges gradually and slowly by decreasing the amount of angulation. As the edges release, allow yourself to drift slightly sideways down the slope. Actually, you will be moving on the bias, so to speak, moving forward and sideways at the same time. That's diagonal sideslipping.

To change this skidding on the bias into a curving sideslip, all you need do is to *increase* the amount of forward lean as you *decrease* the amount of angulation. Automatically, you will begin to turn into the hill. You don't have to try to turn, the skis seem to do the work for you.

Why? Doug Pfeiffer explains this as the friction-gravity principle. When you increase the forward lean, you cause the uphill front edges of the skis to bite just enough more than the edges of the tail of the skis. Therefore, gravity, which is always pulling at you from the side when you traverse, pulls at the tails of the skis and moves them downhill. This creates the effect that you are turning into the hill.

The movements just discussed are crucial. You must learn how to release your edges at will, with both a decrease in angulation and/or a slight rolling out of the ankles. These few movements are what control an estimated eighty per cent of your advanced skiing ability.

Resetting the edges after sideslipping

Practice the curving sideslip on gentle slopes, on steep slopes, at slow speeds, or as fast as you can safely go. Vary the angle of your curve. Lean forward a great deal, to make the tails of your skis come around suddenly. Experiment by releasing your edges more and leaning less forward. After some hours of this type of varied practice, scattered over several days or even weeks of skiing, you will master the art of controlling your edges. Count on at least a total of ten hours of serious practice on this exercise alone.

The curving sideslip, with the addition of an up-unweighting movement, becomes what the American Technique calls the final-form uphill christie. This extra movement makes the releasing of the edges easier, and at the same time prepares a student for complete parallel christies, where unweighting is needed.

To add up-unweighting to the curving sideslip, do the following: Traverse the slope as before, keeping your skis on their edges. Gradually bend the ankles, knees, and waist more than is necessary. Then quickly rise up, increasing the forward pressure and releasing the edges. The sudden up movement momentarily takes the weight off your skis, and the slip will begin effortlessly. *Note:* Do not rise up so suddenly or so much that you lose your position of balanced stance.

Diagonal Sideslipping

THE SEVENTH SECRET:

The Steered Turns

The steered turns, so called because the skis have to be partially pushed around by the feet and legs, are important secrets, because in learning them you learn several fundamentals of ski technique. Mastering these turns teaches you, for instance, the intricacies of weight-shift, counterrotation, and heel-push, in addition to what you have already learned. These additional fundamentals are basic principles of the American Technique and are vital for more advanced skiing. I'll explain them to you now, as I demonstrate the snowplow turn.

The Snowplow Turn

First Drawing. On a smooth-packed slope, about eight to ten degrees, start out from a snowplow position, keeping careful control of your speed.

Second Drawing. To begin a turn to the right, for example, push your left knee forward and in toward the imaginary center of the turn, at the same time exerting an outward pressure on the left heel. As you push the knee forward, you cause your weight to gradually transfer to your left ski, which is called the outside ski of the turn. Notice how my body seems to lean slightly to the outside, creating a slight amount of angulation. As my knee was pushed forward and inward with the twisting pressure on my heel, I forced the left ski to begin to turn. That action is called heel-push.

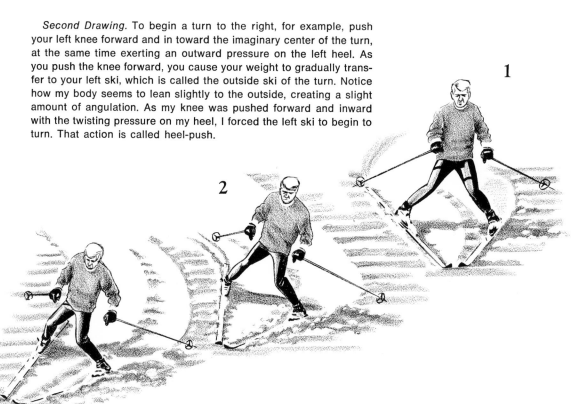

Third Drawing. I continue to apply heel pressure to my left ski. Notice that, as a result, my left shoulder is drawing back somewhat. This motion is called counterrotation, because the movement is opposite, or counter, to the direction of the turn. There is another important thing to watch here. Note how my right knee, the inside knee of the turn, is also pointed forward and in toward the imaginary center of the turn. This action releases the inside edge of that inside ski, allowing it to skim over the snow.

51

The Snowplow Turn

4

Fourth Drawing. I've now begun to link a turn to my left. Notice that I have lost my angulation because my left knee is now no longer bent as deeply as before. I am once again very nearly squared-off and centered to my skis, with my lower shoulder once again brought forward. This has happened because I am beginning to push outward on my right heel, ever so slightly. Notice that at this point my weight is pretty well centered over both skis.

Fifth Drawing. Now you can see how my right knee is just beginning to push forward and in toward the imaginary center of this next turn. Remember, it is always the outside knee of the intended turn which is pushed more forward so that your weight gradually transfers to the outside ski.

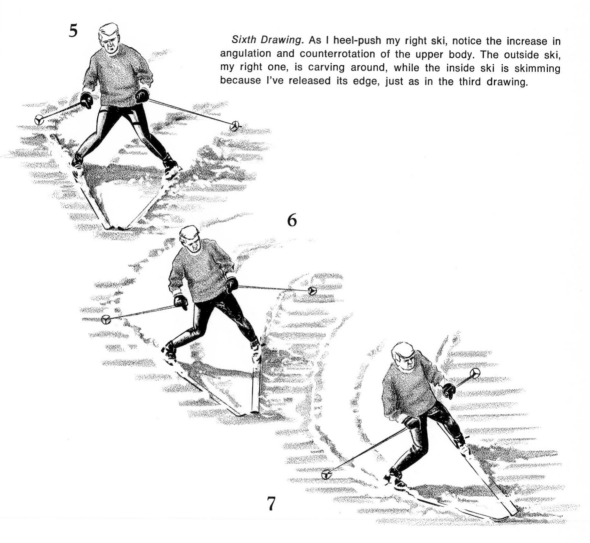

Sixth Drawing. As I heel-push my right ski, notice the increase in angulation and counterrotation of the upper body. The outside ski, my right one, is carving around, while the inside ski is skimming because I've released its edge, just as in the third drawing.

Seventh Drawing. Now that my lower ski has pointed into a new direction, I have begun to settle back to the center of my skis, so that I can either stop, or link another turn into the next direction, my right.

Let's review the three new basic principles and their definitions. Weight-shift is the transfer of your weight from one ski to the other. Counterrotation is the movement of the upper body in the opposite direction to that of the feet and skis. Heel-push, for the time being, is the pushing of one heel so that the ski goes in the direction you wish it to. Weight-shift is nearly always accompanied by a change in angulation. Heel-push is nearly always accompanied by counter-rotation.

The Stem Turn

A stem turn is simply a snowplow turn linking two traverses. No new basic principles are encountered here, except that in order to learn the turn you must learn how to open your skis into a snowplow from a traverse position and then to bring them together again once the turn has been completed. The turn is taught because it is a transition maneuver on the way to the stem christie.

To learn the stem, which is really just a half snowplow done with one ski only, practice on the flat first, then seek out a packed slope and practice from a gentle traverse. A good drill is to simply lift your *upper* ski and place it in a half snowplow, then slide that ski parallel once again. Repeat this maneuver several times while standing still to learn how to place the ski correctly without having to stare at it. The tips should stay fairly close together at all times. Now let's go on to the entire stem turn.

The Stem Turn

First Drawing. Starting from a normal traversing position which will not permit me to go faster than, say, eight miles per hour . . .

Second Drawing. . . . I stem my uphill ski. Notice that my uphill ski has been drawn back slightly, so that my ski tips are even. I've also lost my angulation, so that I'm actually in a pretty good basic snowplow position.

Third, Fourth, Fifth, and Sixth Drawings. During this phase of the turn, which we could call the fall-line phase, the turn is identical to a snowplow turn. For this reason, it is important that you concentrate on maintaining a good snowplow stance throughout.

57

Seventh Drawing. The speed of the stem turn is tightly controlled because of the snowplow. Another way in which speed is controlled at all times is by the angle of the traverse which you take. In this drawing, notice that I am still in a snowplow position. But notice also that my lower ski is now pointing in the direction of a very shallow traverse. At this point, I know from experience that if I close my skis and resume a new traverse I won't pick up any speed for my next turn. This drawing also shows very plainly how my inside knee (my left one) points toward the imaginary center of my turn. Notice how my left ankle has been rolled slightly toward the inside of the turn, so that I can bring down my inside ski . . .

Eighth Drawing. . . . next to the lower one and slightly ahead of it. I am now in a comfortable traverse position in the new direction and am ready to start another stem turn.

The Stem Turn

58

THE EIGHTH SECRET:

The Skidded Turns

Once you master the skidded turns, skiing really becomes exciting. The skidded turns are, of course, the christies. These turns give wings to your feet. You begin to fly instead of merely walk. In a sense, you begin to pull or float your skis around after you from now on, instead of pushing them along in front.

To master the skidded turns another basic principle of the American Technique has to be learned. That's the principle of unweighting by an up-motion. I spoke of this principle when discussing the curving sideslip (see the Sixth Secret). From now on, up-unweighting becomes increasingly important. And so does sideslipping. As a matter of fact, the first exercise often used to lead skiers into the skidded turns is a combination of the curving sideslip and the snowplow, called the snowplow christie. Here is what it looks like.

The Snowplow Christie

1

First Drawing. I'm heading down the fall line in a snowplow. I have neither edged my skis too much nor spread my heels too far apart, so as to gain more speed than normal for a snowplow. I am in a low crouch position. This is so . . .

Second Drawing. . . . I can spring up and forward quickly. The instant I spring, I push hard on the inside edges of my skis, actually *weighting* them for an instant, though it's not evident in this drawing. I have taken advantage of this sudden and very momentary weighting by pushing off my right ski over toward the left one. The instant after I pushed off, the amount of weight pressing on my skis decreased to almost nothing. As a consequence, . . .

2

3

Third Drawing. . . . I begin to turn. Notice the angulation used now. That is, my upper body has begun to lean toward the outside of the turn (my left). And the outside knee has begun to press forward and in toward the imaginary center of the turn. Equally important is the way that I have begun to close my skis. My inside knee (my right one), even though I have brought it closer to the other, has begun to point toward the inside of the turn. This knee action helps to change the edge of that ski from its snowplowing edge to its side-slipping edge. Notice too the slight amount of counterrotation of my shoulders which is counterbalancing the heel-push.

4

Fourth Drawing. My skis are now parallel. I decrease slightly the amount of angulation and carry my weight more evenly between my two skis. Always, however, with more weight on the lower ski.

Fifth, Sixth, and Seventh Drawings. From here on, I control the radius of my skid by making use of the friction-gravity principle. That is, if I press my knees forward more I can allow the tails to skid faster, thereby making a short-radius finish to the turn. Or, I can release the edges ever so slightly and sideslip more. In other words, the rest of this christie, like the end of most christies, is nothing but a curving sideslip.

6

7

The Snowplow Christie

5

When you get on the slopes, don't forget to practice these maneuvers in both directions, otherwise your skiing will become badly lopsided. And especially, spend extra time working out in the direction of your worse side.

The Stem Christie

Now we arrive at the work horse for most recreational skiers, the stem christie. This skidded turn is a speeded-up combination of the snowplow christie and the stem turn. Study these sequence drawings to see what I mean.

First Drawing. Starting from a traverse position on a smooth-packed slope of fifteen to twenty degrees, at such an angle that I go about ten miles per hour, . . .

Second Drawing. . . . I begin to stem my uphill ski just as for a stem turn.

3   *Third Drawing.* Notice the similarity of this drawing to the first one of the snowplow christie. This differs from the stem movement in a stem turn in that I have lowered my body in preparation for . . .

The Stem Christie

4

5

Fourth, Fifth, Sixth, Seventh, Eighth, and Ninth Drawings. . . . the strong, almost explosive up-unweighting movement which you see here. From here on, the turn is conducted exactly as if it were a snowplow christie.

6

7

By the time you have mastered the secrets of the stem christie, consider yourself a good intermediate skier. Though many skiers learn this turn by the end of a week's lessons, generally another week is needed to polish up the details and style and to gain confidence with the turn on slopes of varying steepnesses and varying snow conditions.

8

9

THE NINTH SECRET:

The Parallel Christie

Master the secret of parallel christies and you become a skier in the full sense of the word. Actually, it is not until you can make your skidded turns with the skis kept close together throughout the turn that you will be on the way to becoming an expert. Only the parallel christies permit you to dart quickly in one direction or another, almost at will, almost at any speed, limited only by the speed of your reflexes, your physical condition, and your equipment.

Once you can make consistent parallel christies, the amount of effort expended while skiing is minimal. In a day's skiing you work much less than if you snowplowed or stemmed. The trick lies in finesse—to do just the right amount of the right movement at the right time. And that takes practice.

Before dealing with the completed form of a parallel christie, here is one phase of every downhill turn (except the snowplow turn) which I've not discussed: the change of lead. The leading ski must change its position during a turn. When you recall that the uphill ski always leads when traversing and that you go from one traverse to another during a turn, then the inside ski of that turn must gradually assume the lead position as the turn progresses. During a stem turn, or stem christie, the change of lead begins as you stem the ski, since the stemming is drawn back slightly. Study how the change of lead takes place in the following parallel christie. Notice also how similar this whole turn is to an uphill chistie with unweighting.

First Drawing. Using the same slope as for stem christies, I approach my turning spot from a steeper angle of traverse.

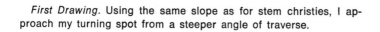

The Parallel Christie

Second Drawing. I prepare for the turn by lowering my body. I have not let this movement affect my skis. Both remain on their uphill edges, and I maintain my original angle of traverse.

Third Drawing. I have sprung up and forward to unweight, while at the same time pushing both heels away from the center of the turn. My outside shoulder has moved back slightly as a result of the heel-push. Notice that my skis have also changed over from resting on their uphill edges to resting on the inside edges of the turn. This change of edges took place because the knees, at the instant my skis were unweighted, were pushed forward and slightly in toward the center of the turn. To compensate for this and to make the transition easier, my upper body had to move slightly from angulating on one side to angulating toward the outside, as you can see in this drawing. This change in angulation helps shift my weight from one ski to another. One final point: Notice that my inside ski has already been brought forward ahead of the other. This change of lead sometimes has to be done consciously; at other times it happens by itself. In any event, the change of lead in a parallel christie should not begin until the moment of unweighting.

69

4

Fourth, Fifth, and Sixth Drawings. From here on, the turn is like ending of a stem christie, except for one difference. In this instance I am shortening the radius of my turn. I make the turn sharper by applying heel-push to the skis as I come off the fall line. This results in more counterrotation of the upper body.

5

6

The Parallel Christie

Seventh Drawing. I have brought the turn to a stop simply by allowing the friction-gravity principle to work on my skis until they point up the hill. From experience I know just how much to let them turn before I re-edge my skis (instructors say "set the edges") for the final stopping.

I could just as well have set my edges in the sixth drawing, thereby preparing myself to immediately link together a parallel christie in the other direction or, simply, to have continued in a traverse until ready to turn again.

7

THE TENTH SECRET:

Wedeln

Wedeln (say VAY-dlen) consists of quick parallel turns one way and then the other, close to the fall line. It is sometimes done with little more than a wiggly track left behind, sometimes with deep looping S's. Wedeln is fun, and done correctly, it allows you to make extremely versatile and useful turns.

But quite frankly, too many of the young men and women who come to our race-training camps wiggle prettily down the fall line of intermediate slopes and are unable to maintain control on steeper faces or to make the well-rounded christies so necessary for giant slalom skiing. For control in the moguls, in deep snow, and for certain combinations of gates in slalom, wedeln works fine, but to become a skillful skier capable of handling fast speeds, slopes without bumps, and long delightful turns, do not neglect the parallel christie—the Ninth Secret.

Wedeln differs from parallel christies in the following respects. Virtually no traverse is evident between turns. If the edges are set, then the traverse is for only the distance of one ski length. Because of this, very quick reflexes and an excellent sense of timing and rhythm are needed, all of which can be developed with practice. As always, learn the basic movements on slopes where you have complete confidence, then gradually progress to more challenging slopes.

One new movement has to be added to your repertoire for you to become an expert at these short-radius turns. That's pole-plant, a quick, almost piston-like jab in the snow with the inside pole to trigger each turn. This action not only helps with the proper timing for the turn, but it also helps to get a quick and efficient up-unweighting, it gives you something to help pivot the turn, and it absorbs some of the shock caused by setting the edges at the conclusion of the last turn.

72

First Drawing. Compare this with the preparation for a parallel christie. My body is lowered to prepare for the up-unweighting, skis on their uphill edges. I have advanced my downhill pole and jabbed it in the snow somewhere to the front of and below my ski boots. Exactly where depends on the length of my pole, the amount of my down-motion while preparing for the upward spring, and my speed. Practice will teach you the best spot for your individual build and equipment. As an approximate guide, the pole should be planted halfway between the tip of the ski and the boot, and about a foot to the side, of the downhill ski. The pole should *always* be planted at the instant you are to spring upward.

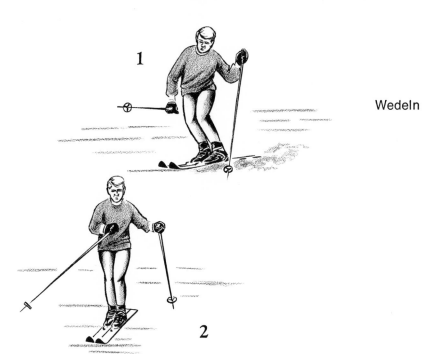

Wedeln

Second Drawing. I have unweighted, heel-pushed the tails of both skis so they turn down into the fall line. The position of my arms and shoulders has changed very little since the last drawing, except for some minor automatic movements necessary to keep the body in balance. To accomplish this balance, flex the muscles of the arm and shoulder so the impact of the pole-plant does not cause either of them to budge backward even an inch. From here on, the turn continues as for any parallel christie, accompanied by angulation and weight-shift.

Wedeln

Third Drawing. To bring the turn around quickly, I have lowered my body position quickly—which, incidentally, helps to keep the ski unweighted—while applying a considerable amount of heel-push and countermotion in the shoulders. I have so timed my movements that my present downhill ski pole is now in a position to be planted, my skis are in a position to set the edges, and I am now ready to spring up and forward into my next turn.

What I have shown here is perhaps the most useful wedeln, called shortswing. On gentle slopes, it is quite possible to go directly from one turn to the next without any intervening setting of the edges. However, such wedeln takes plenty of confidence, since your turns exert no braking action whatsoever on your speed, and the turn becomes more of an exercise in fun than a useful one for avoiding obstacles or maintaining control.

Fourth and Fifth Drawings. The movements here are identical to those of the second and third drawings, only they involve the opposite corresponding parts of the body. Again, I must stress the need for a consistent rhythm for wedeln. The action is turn, turn, turn. No traverse should interrupt the turn.

Summary

I have now taken you through ten secrets, ten steps, as it were, to becoming a good skier. Throughout, I have presented the major points in some detail. I have left out some of the finer points for one reason: If you carefully practice my ten basic secrets, the details will take care of themselves. And, as a second reason, a certified instructor can explain and demonstrate the fine points to you if you need added explanations.

Remember that skiing is an active sport, a doing sport. You cannot learn to ski simply by reading a book. Get out on the slopes and put the information contained in the preceding pages into practice. No matter how good you become, I urge you to spend at least fifteen to thirty minutes each skiing day working deliberately to improve some portion of your technique. You'll find your skiing ability will improve beyond your expectations if you do. I've seen this happen many times.

This phrase may be trite, but it's true: Practice makes perfect, and practice will help you develop rhythm and timing. Good rhythm and timing will help you to improve your balance. Improved balance means improved skill. Improved skill leads to greater safety and greater confidence, and greater confidence leads to greater enjoyment of this great sport. So go to it, skiers of America.

Ski Racing

THE ULTIMATE expression of skill on skis takes place on the race course. Nor is the thrill of racing matched by any other phase of the sport. Although a recreational skier might never have raced, he should try at least one of the "fun" races put on by ski clubs everywhere, once his technique is good enough. There is nothing like the practice of going through a slalom course, where the gates force you to turn at a given place. The training you get from slalom running is invaluable in terms of developing quick reflexes and quick judgment.

Here are a few facts about slalom running and some of the most common patterns of gates used. A gate consists of two poles, each pole having a flag of the same color. You may pass through a gate from either side. You can hit the poles all you like, but if you straddle one and only one foot passes through the gate, you are disqualified. Each gate should be set no less than ten feet wide. No two gates may be closer than two feet.

Here are the basic combinations of gates:

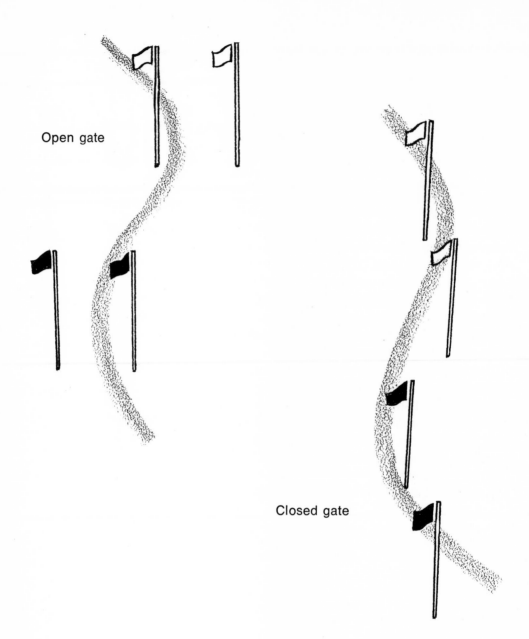

Open gate

Closed gate

78

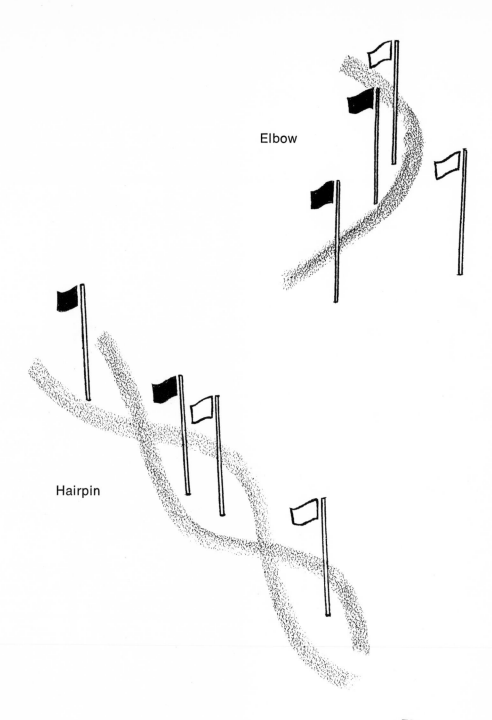

Elbow

Hairpin

79

Four-gate flush

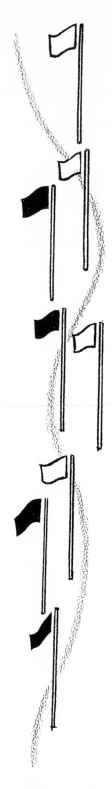

Seelos (or "H")

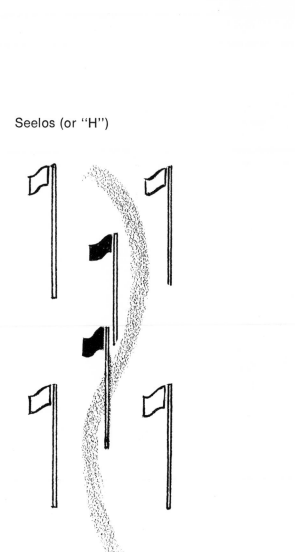

80

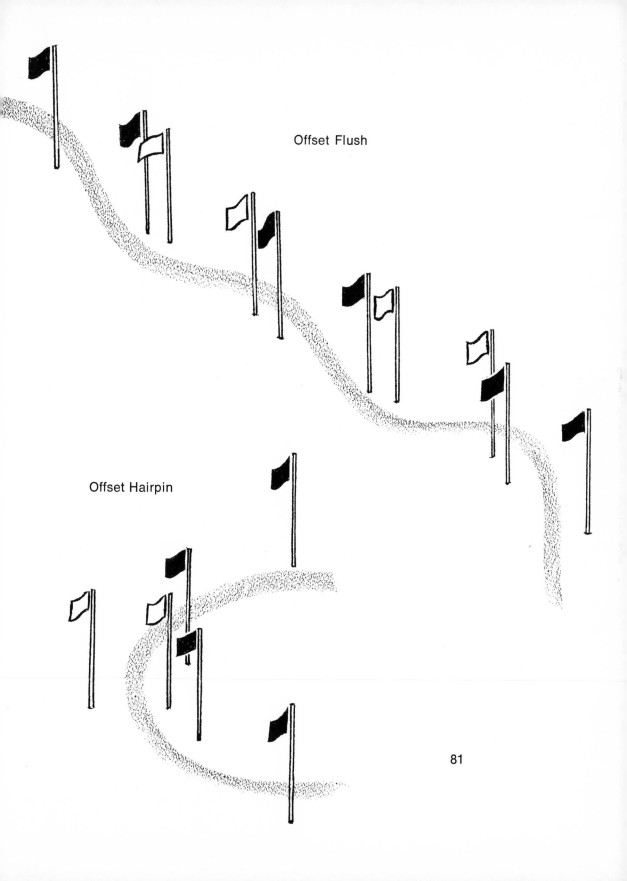

Offset Flush

Offset Hairpin

81

In recent years, America has placed increasing emphasis on ski racing. There are National Junior Championships, National Senior Championships, National Collegiate Championships, and from there up to the FIS World Championships and, ultimately, the Olympic Winter Games.

A great opportunity in ski racing exists today for the youth of America. Several universities and colleges of excellent academic standing provide athletic scholarships to boy and girl skiers who qualify. To mention a few: Chico State College, Chico, California; Colorado University, Boulder, Colorado; Dartmouth College, Hanover, New Hampshire; Denver University, Denver, Colorado; Middlebury College, Middlebury, Vermont; Saint Lawrence University, Canton, New York; Reno University, Reno, Nevada; Western State College, Gunnison, Colorado; Washington University in Seattle, Washington; and Utah University, Salt Lake City, Utah. As the United States Ski Association further organizes the scope of its ski racing program, more and more schools will include skiing on their competitive-sports roster.

Everywhere, junior race programs are thriving. At the moment, one of the temporary problems of the eight various divisions of the USSA is the difficulty of administering properly the burgeoning race programs. As an example of how far we have come in ski racing organization, consider this: in 1964, a year when we sent our nation's best skiers to Innsbruck, Austria, for the Eighth Olympic Winter Games, our budget was $100,000. The year following that, a year when no world championships were scheduled, our budget was increased to $177,000.

American skiers are on the move. Our country is now recognized as an almost equal competitor in World Alpine events. It should not be more than a couple of years before we can field a team of skiers—not just one or two great individuals—who can match the depth and greatness of the Europeans.

Glossary of Basic Principles

ANGULATION

The sideways bending of the torso, away from the slope, or away from the turn, to help keep more of the body weight on the lower ski, or the outside ski, and to counterbalance the control of the edges by the knees.

BALANCED STANCE

The most normal position possible for good, controlled skiing. The ankles, knees, and waist are flexed forward an equal but slight amount, so that the weight of the body can rest comfortably on the ball of each foot, and the hips can be moved at any time to apply more or less forward pressure.

CHANGE OF LEAD

When the inside ski advances so that it will be ahead when a new traverse is reached, during any turn which involves a complete change of direction from one traverse to the next.

COUNTERROTATION

When the lower half of the body, principally the feet, turns in one direction and the upper body is permitted to turn in the opposite direction.

FORWARD LEAN

When the weight of the body is carried on the ball of each foot by leaning the body forward from the ankles, so that at most times the shin is parallel to the backbone.

FRICTION GRAVITY

An increase in forward lean to apply more friction to the front uphill edges of the skis, so that the instant that the edges are released, provided the skier is traversing, gravity will cause the heels of the skis to skid faster, resulting in a curving sideslip. This principle, along with heel-push, is used to vary the radius of any christie.

HEEL-PUSH
A muscular torsion of the lower leg which causes the heels of the skis to be displaced. During this movement the upper body usually rotates in the opposite direction. (See counterrotation.)

NATURAL POSITIONS
Simply the concept that the body should not be forced into unnatural, or extreme, positions for skiing which serve no functional purpose.

POLE-PLANT
When executing christies, to jab the inside ski pole into the snow as an aid to initiating the next turn. The pole action serves as a "trigger" for releasing the turn, in terms of proper timing, as well as an aid to up-unweighting and as a means to absorb some of the body's momentum caused by setting the edges at the end of a turn.

TOTAL MOTION
The concept that, while skiing, the body and all its parts must be in continuous motion in order to maintain good balance. In other words, no single part of the body is moved without compensating adjustments from the remainder of the body.

SETTING THE EDGES
When, at the end of a parallel christie, a good skier re-edges his skis in order to stop all turning action. He would very often use the spring obtained from setting the edges as a means to up-unweight immediately for his next turn.

UP-UNWEIGHTING
When a skier has pushed off his ski edges in a powerful upward motion and the upward thrust generated reduces weight on the snow to practically nothing, making that moment ideal for turning the skis.

WEIGHT-TRANSFER, or WEIGHT-SHIFT

When, as a turn progresses from a traverse into the fall line and then off again, the majority of a skier's weight transfers from his lower ski to the outside ski of the turn, which then becomes the downhill ski for the next traverse.